RESOURCE CENTER
DANVILLE SCHOOL

P9-CFS-046

The Man Who Named the Clouds

Julie Hannah and Joan Holub

Illustrations by Paige Billin-Frye

Albert Whitman & Company, Morton Grove, Illinois

To my daughter and co-author Joan, for all she has taught me.—J. HANNAH

For Woody Davis and Carol Davis.—J. HOLUB

To Diane.—P. BILLIN-FRYE

Library of Congress Cataloging-in-Publication Data

Hannah, Julie.
The man who named the clouds / Julie Hannah and Joan Holub ; illustrations by Paige Billin-Frye.
p. cm.
ISBN-13: 978-0-8075-4974-2 (hardcover)
ISBN-10: 0-8075-4974-6 (hardcover)
1. Howard, Luke, 1772-1864—Juvenile literature. 2. Meteorologists—England—Biography—Juvenile literature.
3. Clouds—Juvenile literature. I. Holub, Joan. II. Billin-Frye, Paige, ill. III. Title.
QC858.H68H36 2006 551.5092—dc22 2006000002

Published simultaneously in Canada by Fitzhenry & Whiteside, Markham, Ontario.

Printed in the United States of America.
10 9 8 7 6 5 4 3 2 1

The design is by Carol Gildar.

For information about Albert Whitman & Company, please visit our web site at www.albertwhitman.com.

Photo Credits:
Page 3: Luke Howard portrait. The picture has been reproduced by kind permission of the Royal Meteorological Society, Reading, England.
Page 15: Montgolfier balloon engraving. National Air and Space Museum, Smithsonian Institution (SI 89-15688).
Pages 1, 19, 27: Luke Howard paintings. Science Museum/Science & Society Picture Library, London, England.
Pages 32, 33, 34, 35: cloud photos. Copyright © 2000 by Keith G. Diem. Used by permission.

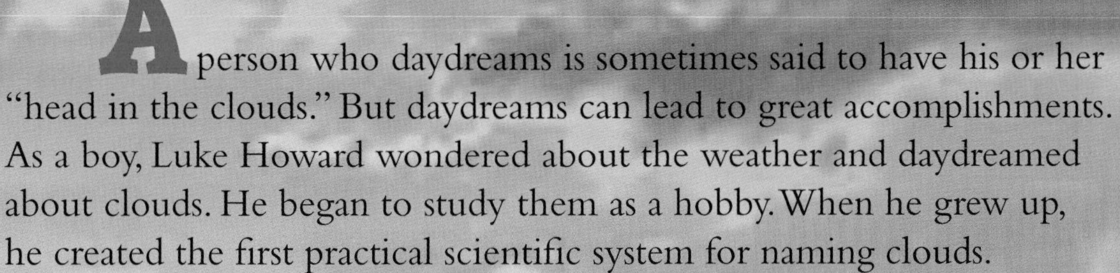

A person who daydreams is sometimes said to have his or her "head in the clouds." But daydreams can lead to great accomplishments. As a boy, Luke Howard wondered about the weather and daydreamed about clouds. He began to study them as a hobby. When he grew up, he created the first practical scientific system for naming clouds.

Luke Howard was born on November 28, 1772, in the city of London, England. When he was young, he noticed there were different kinds of clouds. Some were high and feathery. Some were puffy on top and flat on the bottom. Others looked like gray blankets.

Luke didn't get serious about studying clouds until he was ten years old. That's when he began keeping a weather journal to describe what he saw in the sky.

Luke had three younger brothers, one younger sister, and three older half-brothers. Many of them helped in the family's ironworks business. Their father didn't want his children to be lazy. He taught them the importance of working hard and learning.

When Luke was a boy, it was popular to study science and nature. People wanted to know more about metals and chemicals that might help in manufacturing and making medicines.

And Luke wasn't the only one who was curious about the weather. Many people kept weather journals, hoping to learn more about what caused clouds, rain, and fog. One theory was that clouds were bubbles of air and that the sun's rays gave them the power to float.

My name is Grace. I'm keeping a weather journal like Luke did. It's my science fair project. Once a month during the school year, I'll write these things: the date, the time, the temperature, what kind of weather I see outside, and interesting weather facts.

One thing I've learned is that temperature is measured with a Fahrenheit thermometer in the United States. Most other countries use a Celsius thermometer.

My Weather Journal

September 25 Time: 9:15 A.M.
Temperature: 75° Fahrenheit or 23.9° Celsius
The weather today is: Cloudy

Here's how clouds are made:

1. Sun heats the earth.
2. Water evaporates from the surface of oceans, ponds, lakes, and rivers. Evaporation means a liquid changes to a gas. When water gets warm enough, it evaporates and becomes water vapor, the gas form of water.
3. The warm vapor rises.
4. As the vapor meets higher, cooler air, it condenses into tiny drops of liquid water. Condensation means a gas changes to a liquid.
5. A cloud is made of a bunch of those drops hanging in the sky.

In the 1700s, the causes of weather were a mystery. Sailors and farmers could only watch for signs in nature to help them predict storms.

In dry, sunny weather, they noticed a pine cone's scales opened outward. If its scales folded inward, rain might be on the way.

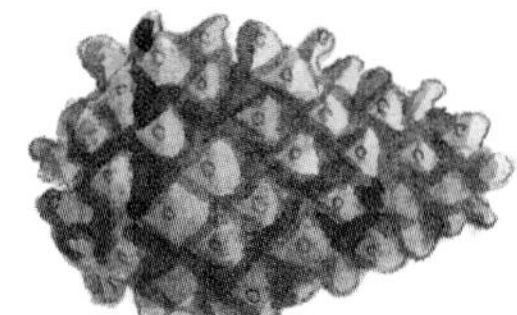

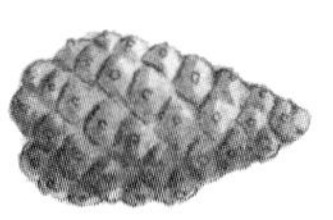

Rhymes like this one also helped in predicting the weather:

Red sky at night, sailor's delight.
Red sky at morning, sailors take warning.

Sailors like red sunsets because it means the air in the west (where the sun sets) is dry. Wind usually moves weather from west to east, so dry air is coming, and the sky will be clear.

If the sunrise sky is red-colored, it means dry air has already moved from the west to the east (where the sun rises). There is a good chance clouds, rain, or even storms will soon come from the west.

People made up sayings comparing clouds to shapes in nature, such as horses' tails or fish scales.

Mares' tails bring storms and gales.

Clouds are blown into wispy, horse-tail shapes by strong, stormy wind.

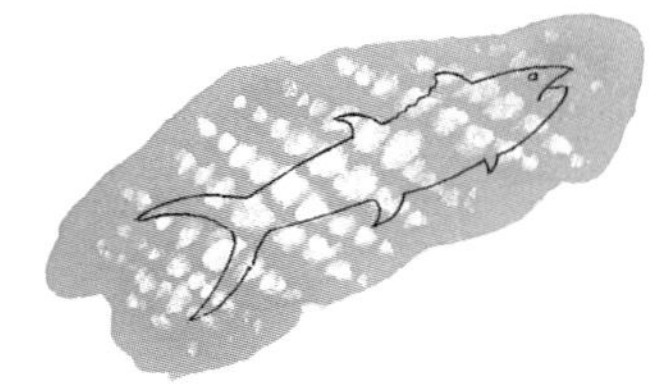

Mackerel sky, mackerel sky,
Never long wet, never long dry.

Clouds shaped like the pattern of scales on a mackerel fish often bring quick showers that come and go.

My Weather Journal

October 23 Time: 9:35 A.M.
Temperature: 68° Fahrenheit or 20° Celsius
The weather today is: Foggy

Today I walked through a cloud on the way to school! Fog is a cloud near the ground. It forms in the same way other clouds do, except for one thing—warm air doesn't rise and get cooled by higher cool air. Instead, the warm air stays low and passes over cool land, making water droplets form. That's why fog clouds are at ground level, instead of high in the sky.

Luke and his family were members of a religion called the Religious Society of Friends, or Quakers. Because Quakers didn't belong to the Church of England, England's main church, they weren't allowed to go to the same schools as people who did. Instead, eight-year-old Luke and his younger brother William attended a Quaker boarding school in Burford, England. They lived at the school year-round, except for a short vacation each summer.

Their teacher was very strict. He smacked students with a cane if they didn't learn quickly enough. Luckily, Luke was a fast learner.

As part of his lessons, Luke had to recite Latin words over and over. This wasn't interesting or fun at the time, but it came in handy years later.

My Weather Journal

November 15 Time: 10:15 A.M.
Temperature: 40° Fahrenheit or 4.4° Celsius
The weather today is: Rainy

I had to play soccer in the mud today. Rain, rain, go away!

Any form of water that falls from the sky is called precipitation. Rain, snow, and hail are all precipitation.

Here's what makes rain:

1. There are millions of tiny water droplets in a cloud. At first, they are too light to fall to earth.
2. Then they begin to stick to tiny bits of dust, salt, or ash in the air.
3. They clump together to form bigger drops.
4. Soon the drops get so heavy that the air can't hold them up anymore.
5. Gravity pulls them back down to earth as raindrops.

What did the boy raindrop say to his new girlfriend?

—I'm falling for you!

In the summer of 1783, when Luke was ten years old, a volcano erupted in Iceland, causing many deaths. Wind blew the ash toward Europe. It mixed with smoke and water vapor to create a dark, stinky fog that hung in the sky over England for months. Luke could hardly see the moon at night or the sun in the daytime!

Dust in the air turned sunrises and sunsets a deep red color. Some people got sick from breathing the dirty air. Plants that didn't get enough sunlight died.

Then, on the night of August 18, Luke and thousands of others saw a fiery meteor flash across the sky! No one knew what might happen next. Some people worried the world was coming to an end. The skies were back to normal by late autumn that year. But the unusual summer weather had made scientists more interested in studying the atmosphere.

Luke had become more interested in the weather, too.

My Weather Journal

December 18   Time: 9:17 A.M.
Temperature: 56° Fahrenheit or 13.3° Celsius
The weather today is: Rainy

A meteorologist is someone who studies changes in the atmosphere that cause weather. The meteorologist on TV said a low-pressure system brought rain to my neighborhood today.

Air pressure is the weight of air pushing against the earth's surface. Cool air is heavier than warm air. So cool air sinks toward the earth and warm air rises away from it.

When cool air sinks, it pushes against, or puts pressure on, the earth's surface. That's a high-pressure system. It often brings dry weather.

When warm air rises, there is less pressure on the earth's surface. That's a low-pressure system. As warm air rises and meets cooler air, rain clouds can form.

A rain guage can measure how much rain has fallen.

You can make your own rain gauge.

What you'll need: a ruler, some clear tape, and a tall glass with straight sides.

What to do:

1. Place the bottom edge of the ruler even with the bottom of the inside of the glass. Tape the ruler to the outside of the glass with the numbers facing outward.
2. Set the glass outside when it looks like it will rain. Record the time and date.
3. Measure the water in the glass at the same time the next day. The number of inches is the amount of daily rainfall.

On September 19, 1783, a balloon called *Le Martial,* which means "the warrior" in French, was launched carrying a duck, a sheep, and a rooster. More than 130,000 people watched, including the king and queen of France.

The year of 1783 was exciting for another reason. Two brothers named Jacques Etienne and Joseph Michel Montgolfier launched the first giant balloons in France. Since clouds could float, the brothers believed a balloon filled with a cloud of smoke might float, too. Perhaps this would allow people to travel long distances high in the sky.

After a series of small balloon experiments, the Montgolfiers launched a fifty-seven-foot-tall hot-air balloon in September, 1783. The decorated balloon made of painted cotton fabric took off from the royal palace at Versailles, France. A basket attached below it contained the very first balloon passengers—a duck, a sheep, and a rooster!

On November 21 the same year, Jean-Francois Pilâtre de Rozier and the Marquis d'Arlandes became the first men to fly in a balloon that wasn't anchored to the ground. The Montgolfiers built this seventy-foot-tall hot-air balloon out of cloth lined with paper. Its passengers sat in a round basket attached by ropes to the bottom of the balloon.

Rozier and Arlandes burned straw and wool on an iron grate under the balloon. Smoke drifted upward through the bottom opening of the balloon, inflating it.

The Montgolfiers thought black smoke caused the balloon to lift, but they were wrong. Heat is what made it rise. When air heats up, it expands and becomes lighter. Lightweight hot air from the fire filled the balloon and allowed it to fly. The passengers rose as high as three thousand feet—over half a mile! They flew for twenty-five minutes, and traveled about five miles over Paris, France.

In the following years, Europeans flocked to watch hot-air balloon launches. Even Luke liked to see balloons take off when he got older. Until airplanes became available in the early 1900s, balloons were the only way scientists could fly high enough to study the atmosphere.

Luke finished school at age fifteen and moved back home to live with his parents. He happily began his weather studies again outside in the family garden.

Twice a day in his journal, he recorded the weather conditions. He used a thermometer to learn the temperature of the air, a weathervane to check the wind direction, a rain gauge to measure the rainfall,

and a barometer to measure the pressure of the atmosphere on the earth's surface.

Luke was still very interested in clouds. Since there were no scientific names for different types of clouds, it was hard to write about them. He painted pictures of clouds instead. These are some of his paintings:

Cloud study by Luke Howard, painted sometime between 1808 and 1811.

Landscape and cloud study by Luke Howard, painted sometime between 1808 and 1811.

Luke's father thought cloud-watching was a waste of time. He wanted his son to learn a trade so he could get a good job. After a few weeks at home, Luke was sent away to work as an apprentice in a Quaker chemist shop, where medicines were made and sold.

Luke worked long hours at the shop for seven years. He didn't have time to study the weather so he was unhappy.

When he finally returned home, he went to work for another chemist for a few months. One day, he cut his hand badly when a glass bottle of poisonous chemicals he was holding broke. After he was well again, his father loaned him the money to open his own small chemist shop.

My Weather Journal

January 24 Time: 9:15 A.M.
Temperature: 23° Fahrenheit or -5° Celsius
The weather today is: Snow

A farmer named Wilson Bentley was born in Vermont in 1865. When he grew up, he was nicknamed "Snowflake Bentley" because he loved snowflakes. He studied and took pictures of them, even though in those days no one else thought they were scientifically important.

Here's how snow is made:

1. Water will freeze at 32° Fahrenheit or 0° Celsius. When the temperature in a cloud is below 32° or 0° Celsius, its water droplets turn into tiny ice crystals.
2. The tiny crystals gather together.
3. The joined crystals become snowflakes. It can take fifty to a hundred crystals to make one snowflake. The drier the air, the smaller the snowflake will be.

Here's how you can compare snowflakes:

1. Take a piece of black construction paper and a magnifying glass outside when it's snowing.
2. Hold the paper flat, facing the sky.
3. Catch several snowflakes on it.
4. Look at them through a magnifying glass —quickly, before they melt!

What's a snowman's favorite shape?

A snow cone.

At age twenty-four, Luke married a woman named Mariabella Eliot. Their first daughter, Mary, was born the following year.

About that time, Luke became the manager of a large chemical factory and shop in the English village of Plaistow. He and his new family moved into a house there. Plaistow wasn't crowded with tall buildings as London had been. There were wide spaces where

Luke could see lots of sky. Upstairs in his new house, he had a weather-watching room with big windows. He filled the shelves with his science books and instruments for recording conditions in the atmosphere.

This was a happy time in Luke's life. He had a good job and he had made friends who liked to study science. Now he could get back to his hobby of weather study.

February 18 Time: 11:05 A.M.
Temperature: 39° Fahrenheit or 3.9° Celsius
The weather today is: Cloudy

Weather is caused when the sun heats the earth. The earth heats nearby air low in the atmosphere. The farther you go from the earth, the cooler the air is, so there's less weather.

We live in the layer of the atmosphere that has almost all of the earth's weather. It's called the troposphere. It starts at ground level and extends eleven miles high over the equator, but it is only five miles high at the North and South poles. Above the troposphere is the stratosphere, where there's hardly any weather at all.

I'm glad we live in the troposphere. I think it would get really boring if we didn't have any weather!

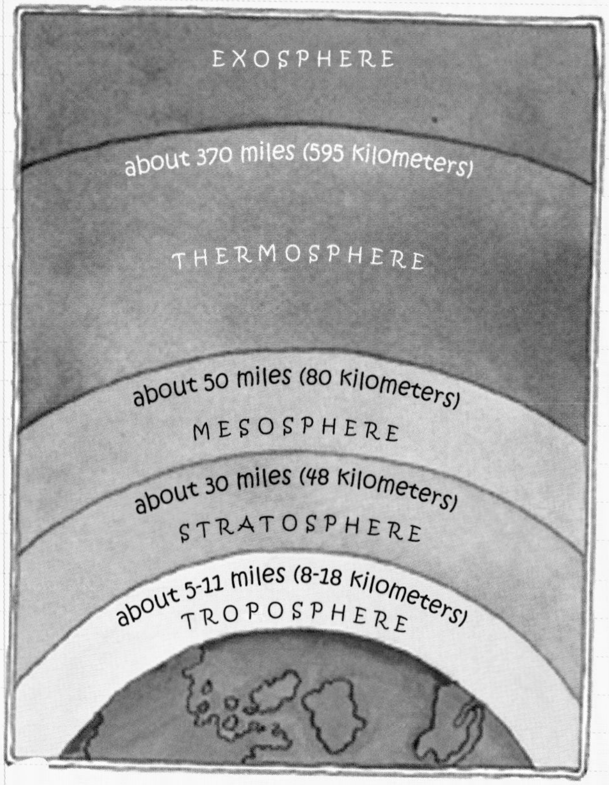

EXOSPHERE
about 370 miles (595 kilometers)
THERMOSPHERE
about 50 miles (80 kilometers)
MESOSPHERE
about 30 miles (48 kilometers)
STRATOSPHERE
about 5-11 miles (8-18 kilometers)
TROPOSPHERE

In what atmospheric layer could a foot of rain fall?

In the toe-posphere.

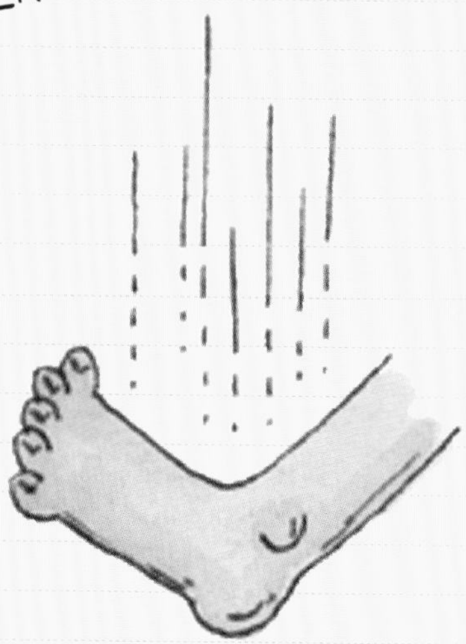

Luke was determined to find new ways to study the weather. In 1796, he joined a club called the Askesian Society. The word *askesian* comes from a Greek word that means "philosophical exercise" or "training."

Most of the club's members were Quakers who wanted to learn about science. They did experiments and brainstormed to try to answer questions about weather, astronomy, electricity, and other branches of science. They wrote their ideas in reports and read them aloud at club meetings held twice a month. At every meeting, each member had to read a paper he had written or pay a fine!

It wasn't easy to discuss clouds because everyone described their shapes differently. Luke knew clouds needed to be classified and named. But scientists had tried this before and failed because their systems weren't exact enough.

Luke studied the work of a Swedish botanist named Carl von Linné, also known as Linnaeus. In 1735, Linnaeus had created a system for scientifically classifying plants and animals using Latin names. This gave Luke an idea for a way to classify clouds.

At a society meeting in 1802, Luke read an essay he'd written called "The Modification of Clouds." (At that time, *modification* meant "classification" or "naming by categories.") In his paper, Luke described three main cloud shapes and gave them Latin names:

Cirrus (a Latin word that means "curl of hair")—"Parallel, flexuous, or diverging fibres, extensible by increase in any or in all directions."

Cumulus (a Latin word that means "heap")—"Convex or conical heaps, increasing upward from a horizontal base."

Stratus (a Latin word that means "layer")—"A widely extended, continuous, horizontal sheet, increasing from below upward."

He also described four other types of clouds, which were combinations of the three main ones: *cirro-cumulus, cirro-stratus, cumulo-stratus,* and *cumulo-cirro-stratus* or *nimbus.* (*Nimbus* means "rain.") Everyone in the Askesian Society was excited about his essay. Finally, someone had a good idea for a system to name clouds!

Light cirro-cumulus below cirrus clouds, painted by Luke Howard sometime between 1803 and 1811.

Stratus clouds near mountains, painted by Luke Howard sometime between 1803 and 1811.

Unknown to Luke, a Frenchman named Jean Baptiste Lamarck had made up another cloud classification system earlier that same year. Lamarck believed there were many cloud types. He planned to name each of them in French, and started with these five:

Nuages en voile (hazy, veil-like clouds)
Nuages attroupes (massed clouds)
Nuages pommeles (dappled clouds)
Nuages balayures (broom-swept clouds)
Nuages groupes (grouped clouds)

At first, there were arguments about which system was better. Was Latin, French, or maybe English the best language for the system?

Latin was the official language of the Roman Empire for over five hundred years, beginning about 31 B.C.E. Because of Rome's widespread influence, many other European languages were based on Latin. So scientists pointed out that people would probably understand Latin cloud names more easily than French ones.

Latin	Italian	Spanish	French	English
nubes	nùvola	nube	nuage	cloud
nebula	nébbia	niebla	brouillard	fog
sol	sole	sol	soleil	sun
tonitrus	tuòno	trueno	tonnerre	thunder
ventus	vènto	viento	vent	wind

Besides, Linnaeus had already succeeded in using a Latin system to classify animals and plants.

In 1803, Luke's essay was printed in a magazine many scientists read and trusted called *Philosophical Magazine.* Soon his cloud-naming system became more popular than Lamarck's.

My Weather Journal

March 21 Time: 9:47 A.M.
Temperature: 62° Fahrenheit or 16.7° Celsius
The weather today is: Windy

Wind is moving air. Here's what causes it:

1. The sun heats the earth.
2. The earth heats the nearby air, making it lighter.
3. The light, warm air rises.
4. Heavy, cool air rushes down from higher in the sky to take the place of the warm air. Wind usually blows from high-pressure areas to low-pressure areas.

Why is the wind never invited to a cloud's birthday party?

Because it always blows out the candles on the cake.

Luke's essay was printed and sold in bookstores. His cloud-naming system appeared in the *Encyclopedia Americana* in the early 1800s.

Still, scientists argued about his system. Was it really possible there were only seven cloud types as Luke claimed? Although some people proposed different classification ideas, Luke never changed his list of seven cloud types. But, over time, others did.

In 1896, an important conference about weather was held in Paris, France. Scientists who attended agreed on a list of ten types of clouds. Each cloud type was given a name based on its shape and the height of its base. Five of Luke's original cloud names were used on the new list. The other five were combinations or revisions of his cloud names.

Today, the World Meteorological Organization (WMO), an agency of the United Nations located in Switzerland, is the authority on clouds and weather. The WMO still uses these ten basic cloud names, described on the following pages.

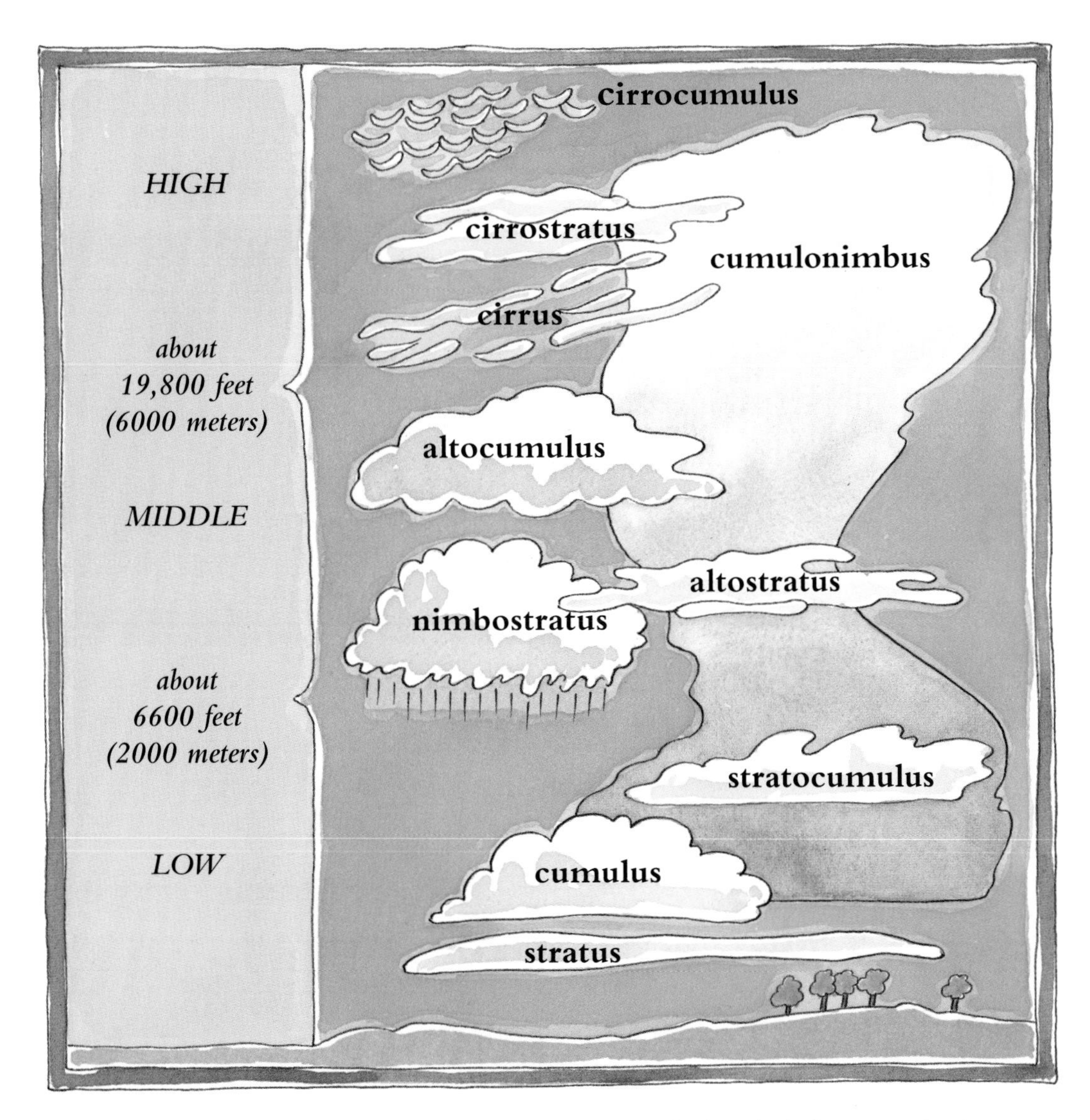

You can tell different kinds of clouds apart by their shape and by how high they are in the sky. The sky often contains a mix of the ten types of clouds.

Cirrus, cirrocumulus, and *cirrostratus:* clouds that are high in the sky. These cloud types are made of ice crystals because the air nearby is so cold.

Cirrus —Very high, thin, wispy clouds with curly ends; sometimes called "mares' tails."

Cirrocumulus – Patches of clouds that form a pattern of waves and ripples; sometimes called "mackerel" clouds.

Cirrostratus –Very thin sheets of clouds; sometimes called "bedsheet" clouds.

Altocumulus, altostratus, and *nimbostratus:* clouds that are in the middle of the sky. Rain or snow may fall from this group of clouds.

Altocumulus – Puffy clouds that sometimes look like rows of cotton balls.

Altostratus – Gray sheets of clouds through which sunlight can often be seen.

Nimbostratus – Heavy, dark clouds that are not puffy and through which sunlight usually cannot be seen.

Stratocumulus, stratus, and *cumulus:* clouds that are the low in the sky.

Stratocumulus – Clouds with bulges and rolls that sometimes form into rows.

Stratus – Foggy cloud layers that look like blankets covering the sky.

Cumulus – Clouds that look like cauliflower or popcorn balls, with puffy tops and flatter bottoms. They change shape quickly and are usually white against a blue sky.

Cumulonimbus: a low cloud that can stretch high in the sky.

Cumulonimbus – Giant clouds that are often flat and wide on top. They can bring thunder, lightning, and rain.

Other Latin words are sometimes added to the ten cloud names to modify them. For instance, an altocumulus cloud shaped like a castle turret is called an *altocumulus castelanus* cloud.

My Weather Journal

April 16 Time: 9:18 A.M. Temperature: 69° Fahrenheit or 20.6° Celsius
The weather today is: Thunderstorms with cumulonimbus clouds

People called Vikings lived in Scandinavia about a thousand years ago. They believed a god named Thor made thunder by banging a big hammer in the sky. But thunder is really the sound that lightning makes. Lightning is a huge electric spark caused when air and moisture move around in the clouds. You see lightning flash before you hear its thunder because light travels faster than sound.

How far away is the lightning from you?

1. After you see lightning flash, start counting the number of seconds that pass.
2. When you hear thunder, stop counting.
3. Divide the number of seconds you counted by five. That's the number of miles between the lightning and you.

Though studying weather was Luke's passion most of his life, it remained only a hobby. He earned his living as a chemist. In 1807, he opened a large chemist shop and laboratory in Stratford, England, called Luke Howard & Company.

As news of his cloud-naming system spread, scientists asked him to give speeches about weather. Luke's weather observations were published in 1818 in two book volumes called *The Climate of London*. *Seven Lectures on Meteorology,* his textbook about the science of meteorology, was published in 1837.

Many people admired and praised Luke, but he always tried to be a good Quaker and stay humble.

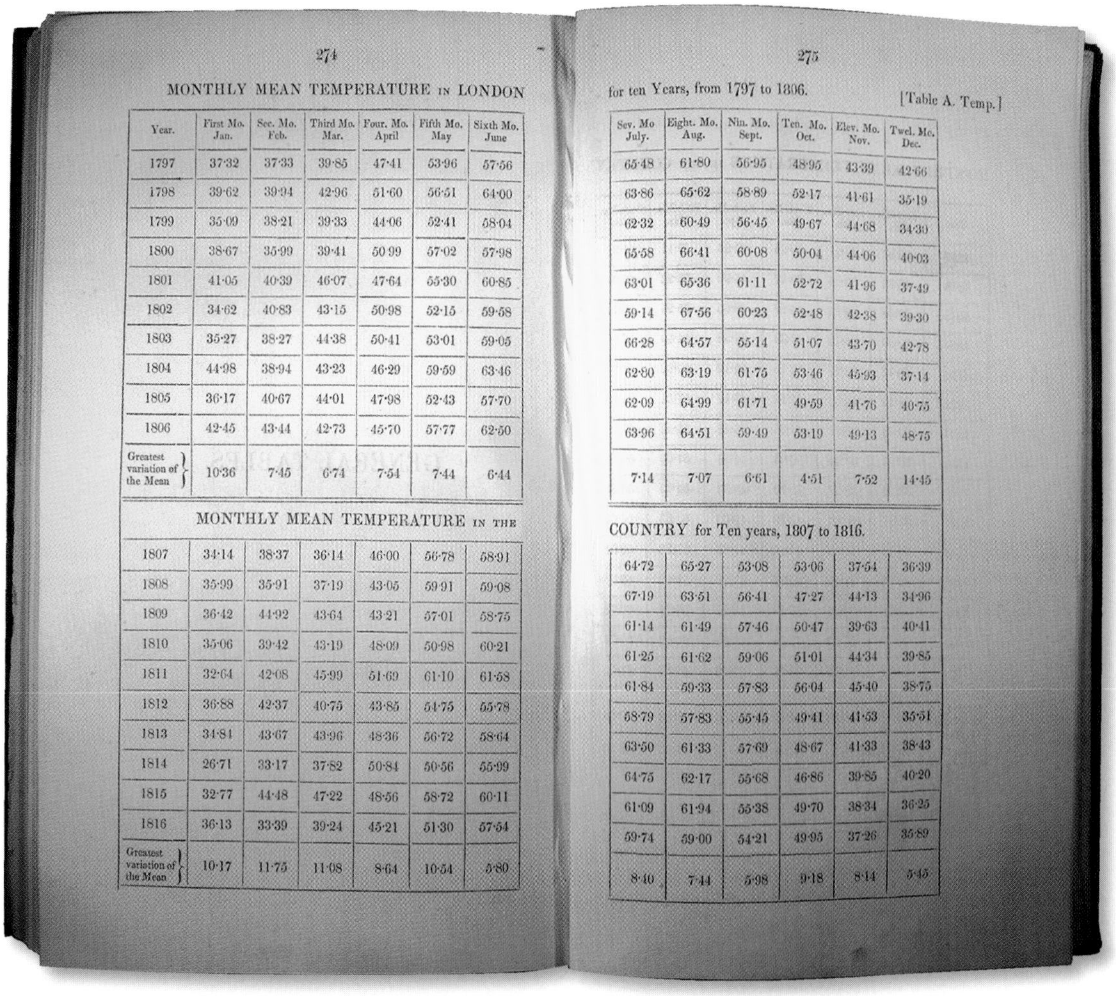

274

MONTHLY MEAN TEMPERATURE IN LONDON

Year.	First Mo. Jan.	Sec. Mo. Feb.	Third Mo. Mar.	Four. Mo. April	Fifth Mo. May	Sixth Mo. June
1797	37·32	37·33	39·85	47·41	53·96	57·56
1798	39·62	39·94	42·96	51·60	56·51	64·00
1799	35·09	38·21	39·33	44·06	52·41	58·04
1800	38·67	35·99	39·41	50 99	57·02	57·98
1801	41·05	40·39	46·07	47·64	55·30	60·85
1802	34·62	40·83	43·15	50·98	52·15	59·58
1803	35·27	38·27	44·38	50·41	53·01	59·05
1804	44·98	38·94	43·23	46·29	59·59	63·46
1805	36·17	40·67	44·01	47·98	52·43	57·70
1806	42·45	43·44	42·73	45·70	57·77	62·50
Greatest variation of the Mean	10·36	7·45	6·74	7·54	7·44	6·44

MONTHLY MEAN TEMPERATURE IN THE

1807	34·14	38·37	36·14	46·00	56·78	58·91
1808	35·99	35·91	37·19	43·05	59 91	59·08
1809	36·42	44·92	43·64	43·21	57·01	58·75
1810	35·06	39·42	43·19	48·09	50·98	60·21
1811	32·64	42·08	45·99	51·69	61·10	61·58
1812	36·88	42·37	40·75	43·85	54·75	55·78
1813	34·84	43·67	43·96	48·36	56·72	58·64
1814	26·71	33·17	37·82	50·84	50·56	55·99
1815	32·77	44·48	47·22	48·56	58·72	60·11
1816	36·13	33·39	39·24	45·21	51·30	57·54
Greatest variation of the Mean	10·17	11·75	11·08	8·64	10·54	5·80

275

for ten Years, from 1797 to 1806. [Table A. Temp.]

Sev. Mo July.	Eight. Mo. Aug.	Nin. Mo. Sept.	Ten. Mo. Oct.	Elev. Mo. Nov.	Twel. Mo. Dec.
65·48	61·80	56·95	48·95	43·39	42·66
63·86	65·62	58·89	52·17	41·61	35·19
62·32	60·49	56·45	49·67	44·68	34·30
65·58	66·41	60·08	50·04	44·06	40·03
63·01	65·36	61·11	52·72	41·96	37·49
59·14	67·56	60·23	52·48	42·38	39·30
66·28	64·57	55·14	51·07	43·70	42·78
62·80	63·19	61·75	53·46	45·93	37·14
62·09	64·99	61·71	49·59	41·76	40·75
63·96	64·51	59·49	53·19	49·13	48·75
7·14	7·07	6·61	4·51	7·52	14·45

COUNTRY for Ten years, 1807 to 1816.

64·72	65·27	53·08	53·06	37·54	36·39
67·19	63·51	56·41	47·27	44·13	34·96
61·14	61·49	57·46	50·47	39·63	40·41
61·25	61·62	59·06	51·01	44·34	39·85
61·84	59·33	57·83	56·04	45·40	38·75
58·79	57·83	55·45	49·41	41·53	35·51
63·50	61·33	57·69	48·67	41·33	38·43
64·75	62·17	55·68	46·86	39·85	40·20
61·09	61·94	55·38	49·70	38·34	36·25
59·74	59·00	54·21	49·95	37·26	35·89
8·40	7·44	5·98	9·18	8·14	5·45

Some of the temperature records Luke Howard kept at Plaistow were published in a book he wrote called *The Climate of London*.

Luke and Mariabella had a long marriage, and he enjoyed spending time with their eight children. Two of his sons worked in his chemist shop when they grew up. Luke's sister, Elizabeth, said that in his later years, he was "always having some of his children and grandchildren with him."

Even as a very old man, Luke loved to watch the sky. By the time he died on March 21, 1864, at the age of ninety-one, he and his cloud-naming system were famous around the world.

My Weather Journal

May 18
Time: 10:15 A.M.
Temperature: 75° Fahrenheit or 23.9° Celsius
The weather today is: Blue skies with cumulus and cirrus clouds

The clouds are changing shape quickly today. Air inside and outside of clouds is always moving. Some clouds, such as stratus, can last for days. Cumulus clouds usually last less than an hour or so. Sometimes a cloud will come and go in ten minutes!

Watching the clouds move helps meteorologists tell what the weather will be. Satellite photos and instruments that measure the height and motion of clouds help them figure out the path of storms. But clouds don't always do what's expected, so it's still hard to predict the weather right every time.

When is the sky like a boy's parent?
When it has a sun.

Amazing weather that really happened:

- France got some of the weirdest weather ever in 1833. Frogs fell from the sky during a rainstorm! They had probably been picked up from lakes or rivers by a tornado-like waterspout, which then dropped them over land. Snakes and fish have also been known to fall during rainstorms in other areas.
- On Kauai Island in Hawaii, it rains as many as 350 days a year.
- Mawsynram, India, holds the world record for the most rainfall—467 inches (1186 centimeters) a year!

- The lowest temperature ever recorded was -128.6° Fahrenheit or -89.2° Celsius at Vostok, Antarctica, on July 21, 1983.
- Fifteen-inch-wide (38 centimeters) snowflakes fell at Fort Keogh, Montana, on Jan 28, 1887. They were bigger than plates!
- In 1998-99, a record amount of snow fell in one year at Mount Baker in Washington state—95 feet (29 meters)!
- The fastest non-hurricane wind on record blew at a top speed of 231 miles (372 kilometers) per hour on April 12, 1934, at Mount Washington in New Hampshire.
- The sun doesn't shine at all for 176 days of the year at the North Pole or for 182 days of the year at the South Pole.

I'm glad the sun is shining in my neighborhood now.

Time to go play soccer!

Selected Bibliography

Allaby, Michael. *How the Weather Works.* New York: The Reader's Digest Association, Inc./ London: Dorling Kindersley Ltd., 1995.

DeMillo, Rob. *How Weather Works.* Emeryville, California: Ziff-Davis Press, 1994.

DePaola, Tomie. *The Cloud Book.* New York: Holiday House, 1975.

Galiano, Dean. *Clouds, Rain, and Snow.* New York: The Rosen Publishing Group, 2000.

Hamblyn, Richard. *The Invention of Clouds.* New York: Farrar, Straus and Giroux, 2001.

Harper, Suzanne. *Clouds: From Mare's Tails to Thunderheads.* New York: Franklin Watts, 1997.

Howard, Elizabeth. "Fragments of Family History," 1862. (http:www.lordsmeade.freeserve.co.uk/background.htm.)

Howard, Elizabeth. "Personal Memoranda," 1862. (http:www/lordsmeade.freeserve.co.uk/background.htm.)

Howard, Luke. *The Climate of London: Deduced from Meterorological Observations, Made in the Metropolis and at Various Places around It.* 2nd ed., 3 vol. London: Harvey and Darton, 1833.

Howard, Luke. *Essay on the Modifications of Clouds.* 1803. Reprint, with *The Language of the Clouds* by Ernst Lehrs. Fair Oaks, California: Rudolf Steiner College Press/ St. George Publications, 1987.

Jackson, Donald Dale. *The Aeronauts.* Alexandria, Virginia: Time-Life Books, 1980.

Marion, Fulgence. *Wonderful Balloon Ascents.* France: 1870. Translated by Jim Henderson. Project Gutenberg Literary Archive Foundation, © 2003-2006.

Perry, Phyllis J. *Ballooning.* New York: Franklin Watts, 1996.

Staub, Frank. *The Kids' Book of Clouds & Sky.* New York: Sterling Publishing Co., 2003.

Stephens, Graeme L. *"The Useful Pursuit of Shadows."* American Scientist 91 (September-October 2003): 442-49.

Website: http://www.cloudman.com/luke/luke_howard.htmw